# DISCOVERY READERS

# What Do Animals Do in Winter?

### By Melvin and Gilda Berger
### Illustrated by Susan Harrison

ideals children's books™
Nashville, Tennessee

This edition first published in 2002.

The authors, artist, and publisher wish to thank the following for their invaluable advice and instruction for this book:

Jane Hyman, B.S., M.Ed. (Reading), M.Ed. (Special Needs), C.A.E.S. (Curriculum, Administration, and Supervision)

Rose Feinberg, B.S., M.Ed. (Elementary Education), Ed.D. (Reading and Language Arts)

R.L. 2.3 Spache

ISBN 0-8249-5314-2

Published by Ideals Children's Books
An imprint of Ideals Publications
A division of Guideposts
535 Metroplex Drive, Suite 250
Nashville, Tennessee 37211
www.idealsbooks.com

Text copyright © 1995 by Melvin and Gilda Berger
Illustrations copyright © 1995 by Ideals Publications, a Division of Guideposts

Printed and bound in Mexico by RR Donnelley.

Library of Congress Cataloging-in-Publication Data

Berger, Melvin
    What do animals do in winter? : how animals survive the cold / by Melvin and Gilda Berger; illustrated by Susan Harrison.
        p. cm.—(Discovery readers)
    Includes index.
        1. Animals—Wintering—Juvenile literature. [1. Animals—Wintering.
2. Winter] Berger, Gilda. II. Harrison, Susan J., ill. III. Title. IV. Series.
QL753.B37        1995
591.54'3—dc20                                95–10419
                                                CIP
                                                AC

What Do Animals Do in Winter? is part of the Discovery Readers™ series. Discovery Readers™ is a trademark of Ideals Publications, a Division of Guideposts.

Cover design by Jenny Hancock

10 9 8 7 6 5 4 3 2 1

In winter some places turn very cold.
  Icy winds blow.
  The trees have no leaves.
  The flowers are gone.
  Ponds freeze over.
  Snow covers the ground.
  And most animals are missing.

3

# What do the animals *do* when it gets very cold?

4

**Animals travel.**

Some animals migrate (MI-grate).
That means they leave their homes
and travel to other places.
They go to places
—where the weather is warm
—where they can find food.
Here they stay until spring.

In spring the animals return home.
The weather is warm now.
Everything is starting to grow again.
The animals stay here until winter
    comes.
Then they migrate again.

Some kinds of birds migrate.
They know when it's time to go.
The weather turns chilly.
The days grow shorter.

The birds gather together.
They sit in groups on telephone
    wires and in trees.
Soon they are ready to fly away.
Off they go.

Some birds fly far away.
Other birds go only a short distance.

Robins migrate.
But they do not go very far.
They go just far enough to find food.

Other birds go much farther.
Warblers fly over 2,000 miles.

The Arctic tern migrates the farthest.
This seabird lives near the North Pole.
In winter it flies 11,000 miles south.
Finally it reaches the South Pole.
In spring it flies all the way back.

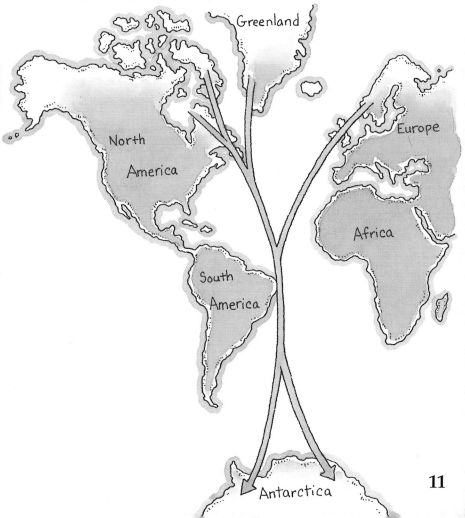

Greenland

North
America

Europe

Africa

South
America

Antarctica

Monarch (MON-ark) butterflies live
    in Canada.
They also go south in winter.
But first they must get ready.
In fall they gather in huge numbers.
Then they fly away.

Some fly to Florida.
Some fly to California.
Some fly as far south as Mexico.

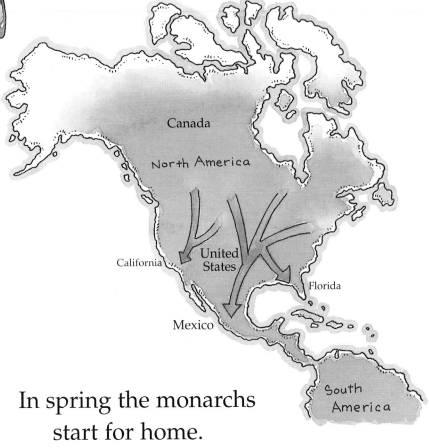

In spring the monarchs
    start for home.
Along the way they lay eggs and die.
Soon the eggs hatch.
The new butterflies finish the trip.

Reindeer (RAIN-deer) live in cold
     lands.
Some live on mountains.
In winter the snow piles up.
It buries the grasses and leaves.
The reindeer have little to eat.

Each year the reindeer migrate.
Thousands may travel together.
They go to places with less snow.

They go into valleys.
There they find plants to eat.
They go back home in the spring.

Some whales live in cold ocean
    waters.
There's lots to eat here.
But in winter the waters freeze over.
So the whales migrate.

The whales go to warmer waters.
The mothers have their babies.
By spring the young whales have
    grown quite big.
They swim back home with their
    mothers.

**What *else* do animals do when it
gets very cold?**

**Animals sleep.**

Some animals hibernate (HI-bur-nate)
    in winter.
That means they go to sleep.
They find places
    —where they can stay warm
    —where they will feel safe.

Groundhogs hibernate in winter.
They sleep in nests.
Their nests are inside tunnels under
    the ground.

All spring and summer the
    groundhogs are busy.
They eat and eat.
They find plants and grass
    everywhere.
Soon they are big and fat.

In fall the groundhogs get ready to
hibernate.
They line their nests with grass.
Then they curl up.
They wrap their tails around
themselves.
And they go to sleep for the winter.

Groundhogs may sleep for six
months.
They do not eat.
They live off the fat in their bodies.
They lose about half of their weight.

In spring the groundhogs come out
of their tunnels.
They look around for food.
The males and females mate.
Four weeks later, baby groundhogs
are born.

Bats also hibernate.
But they hibernate in caves.
They hang upside down.
They wrap their wings around
themselves.
That keeps them warm while they
sleep.

Frogs and turtles hibernate too.
So do snakes, snails, and some kinds
   of squirrels.
These animals lie very still.
They breathe slowly.
They grow cold and stiff.
And they don't eat anything all
   winter.

turtle

snail

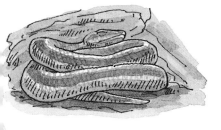

snake

frog

Bears hibernate in caves or in holes in
the ground.
But they are light sleepers.
They may wake to look for food.
Then they go back to sleep.

Raccoons also sleep through the cold
  winters.
They make their dens in hollow trees,
  logs, or stumps.
On warmer days, they might wake
  up and look for food.
Then they go back to their dens.

Chipmunks are light sleepers too.
All spring and summer they gather
food.
They store it in tunnels under the
ground.

In fall the chipmunks get ready for
winter.
They cover the food with dried grass.
The dried grass is their bed.
They climb on top and go to sleep.

In winter the chipmunks wake once
    in a while.
They are hungry.
So they reach under their bed for a
    snack.
Then they go back to sleep.

**What *else* do animals do when it
    gets very cold?**

**Animals hide.**

Some animals hide in winter.
They hide in their dens or nests.
Here they keep warm.

Some kinds of squirrels hide in
winter.

Sometimes the squirrels come out.
They look for something to eat.
Often they are lucky.
They find the nuts they hid in fall.
They find the food people put in
    feeders.

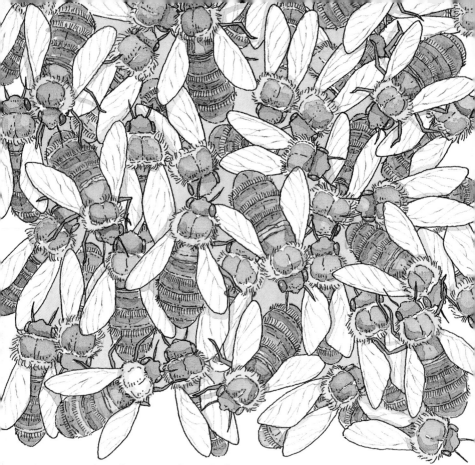

Bees hide in their hives in winter.
Honeybees pile up in one big ball.
The center ones wiggle to keep warm.
The outside ones push their way
    inside.
The bees eat the honey they made in
    the summer.
On warm days some fly out
    to find more food.

Ants hide in their nests under the
   ground.
Their nests have many rooms.
In winter the ants live in the deepest
   rooms.
They eat the food they stored.

Beavers hide in their lodges.
Lodges are houses that beavers build.
The houses are above the water.
They are warm and dry.

All summer the beavers are busy.
They cut down trees with their teeth.
They store the pieces inside their
    lodges.

In winter the beavers stay inside.
They eat the bark from the wood they
    stored.

lodge

Caterpillars (KAT-uh-pil-urs) make
houses called cocoons.
The cocoons hang from branches.
The caterpillars stay warm and dry
inside.

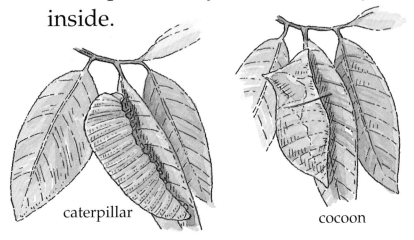

caterpillar                    cocoon

In spring they come out as butterflies.

butterfly

A bird called a ptarmigan (TAR-mi-
gun) also changes its color.
Most of the time its feathers are
brown and black.
But in winter its feathers turn white.
The white feathers hide the bird in
the snow.

ptarmigan

Foxes don't hibernate.
They don't migrate.
They don't hide.
Most don't change color.
**What do *they* do when it gets very
cold?**

In winter foxes grow extra fur.
The fur traps air.
The layer of air keeps the foxes warm.
All winter the foxes hunt as usual.
They catch mice, chickens, rabbits,
and birds.

Here's a surprise.
In different parts of the world, it is
    cold at different times of the year.
In some places it is cold in December.
In other places it is cold in July.

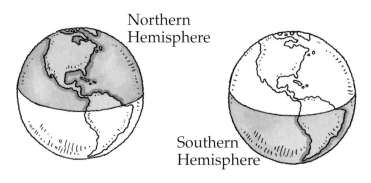

Northern Hemisphere

Southern Hemisphere

The earth is divided into two parts.
The top part is called the Northern
    Hemisphere.
Some places here have winter weather
    from December to early March.

The bottom part of the earth is called
    the Southern Hemisphere.
Some places here have winter weather
    from late June to early September.

# The green areas on this map are warm all year round.

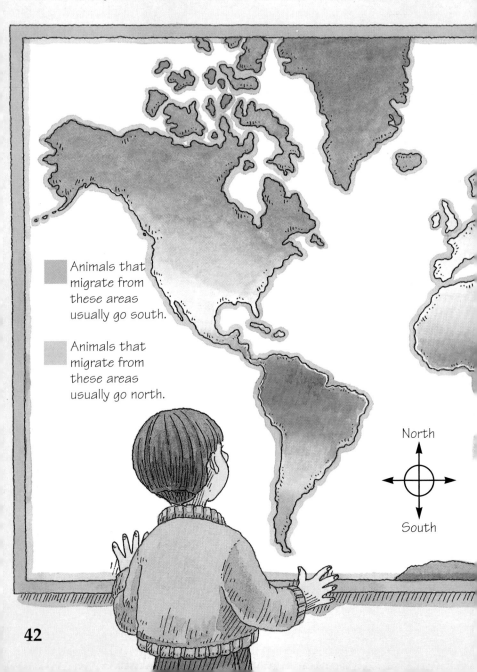

Animals that migrate from these areas usually go south.

Animals that migrate from these areas usually go north.

North

South

But wherever winter weather comes,
animals must find ways to survive.

# So what do animals *do* in winter?

Some animals travel.

Some animals sleep.

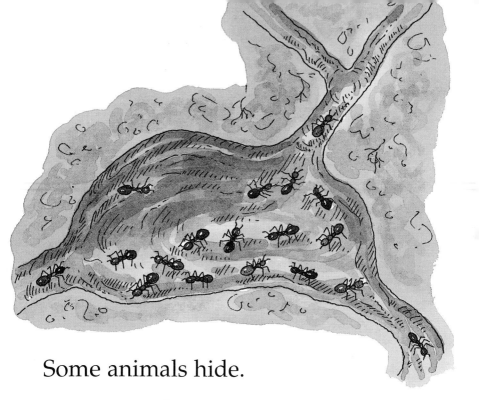

Some animals hide.

Some animals change color.

Humans also live in places that get
    very cold.
**What do *they* do in winter?**

A few people migrate to where it is
   warm.

Most do not.

They spend more time inside their
   warm houses.

They wear extra layers of clothing.

They have fun in the ice and snow!

# Index